YOUR KNOWLEDGE HAS VALUE

- We will publish your bachelor's and master's thesis, essays and papers

- Your own eBook and book - sold worldwide in all relevant shops

- Earn money with each sale

Upload your text at www.GRIN.com
and publish for free

Environmental Crime and Biodiversity. A Maltese Context

Kimberley Bartolo

Bibliographic information published by the German National Library:

The German National Library lists this publication in the National Bibliography; detailed bibliographic data are available on the Internet at http://dnb.dnb.de.

ISBN: 9783346308504
This book is also available as an ebook.

© GRIN Publishing GmbH
Nymphenburger Straße 86
80636 München

Print and binding: Books on Demand GmbH, Norderstedt, Germany
Printed on acid-free paper from responsible sources.

The present work has been carefully prepared. Nevertheless, authors and publishers do not incur liability for the correctness of information, notes, links and advice as well as any printing errors.

GRIN web shop: https://www.grin.com/document/958696

Environmental Crime and Biodiversity: A Maltese Context

The interplay between Environmental Law and Policy

Kimberley Bartolo

Table of Contents

The interplay between Environmental Law and Policy

Examining the current regulatory framework and its effectiveness in:

- safeguarding and enhancing the environment; preventing or decreasing environmental crime;
- ensuring the sustainable development of Malta's urban, rural, costal and marine area.

1.1 Introduction

Safeguarding the environment should be a major concern for every human being. This is because if it is not protected, future generations would not be able to enjoy such a planet (Betz, 2016). There are various laws and policies which regulate and enforce the protection of the environment, with the help of several legal tools. Both people and organizations, as well as the government, should focus upon safeguarding the environment in the best ways possible (Bing-Yuk, 2009). In fact, Chapter 549 of the Laws of Malta states that, "it shall be the duty of every person ... to protect the environment" and, "it shall be the duty of the Government to protect the environment for the benefit of the present and future generations" (Chapter 549: Environment Protection Act, 2016).

1.2 The interplay between Environmental Law and Policy

With the word interplay, one understands the manner in which our legal tools can properly implement the safeguarding of the environment. The two principle tools with regards to safeguarding the environment are the; legal regime and, the policy framework. These tools work interchangeably to enhance and ensure the protection of the environment (Kiyoung, 2014).

Prior the split of the Malta Environment and Planning Authority (MEPA) in 2016 ("Split of MEPA", 2017), the main piece of legislation that tackled the environment in Malta, was Chapter 504: The Environment and Development Planning Act, from the Laws of Malta (2014). Today, this entity has been split into two autonomous and independent authorities which are the Environmental Resources Authority (ERA) and the Planning Authority (PA) (ERA, n.d.). The main focus of the ERA is upon safeguarding the environment for a more sustainable quality of life (ERA, n.d.). While, the PA's vision and mission is upon making the Maltese islands a better place to live in by regulating development, on behalf of the community (Planning Authority, 2016). The two primary laws which regulate the environment's protection and development nowadays are; Chapter 549: Environment Protection Act (2016), and Chapter 552: Development Planning Act (2016), from the Laws of Malta. Briefly, the law of Chapter 549 states that every individual, organization, entity, and also the government, has the duty to prevent and use necessary remedies in order to protect the environment (Chapter 549, 2016). Whilst, Chapter 552 focuses on having sustainable development in order to enhance the quality of life, for both present and future generations (Chapter 552, 2016).

Furthermore, the other legal tool which sustains to the protection of the environment is the policy framework. It is aimed to further the proper implementation of the law in various sectors. The main document, within the local context, of the policy framework is the Strategic Plan for Environment and Development, SPED in short, in which a number of policies about the safeguarding of the environment are cited. SPED uses an approach where strategic planning is developed to surround the concept of spatial planning. It covers the sustainable and management use, of both sea and land resources in an integrated manner. It calls for the rehabilitation of the natural environment, and the protection and enhancement of the Maltese landscape as well as its rural recreational resources (Planning Authority, 2015). This policy was approved in 2015 by the parliament, and is to remain in action until 2020 (ERA, 2014). This plan, replaced the 1992 Structure Plan for the Maltese islands, since it was developed in a context in which development was broadly initiated without any strategic guidance or, without thoughtful considerations of its impacts, on the environment (SPED, 2015). Within the SPED, there are found several subsidiary plans. These subsidiary plans tackle the specific development planning requirements within a particular area (Chapter 552, 2016). One example of a subsidiary plan is the local plans (LP). These LPs lay down specific planning parameters, for different areas around Malta and Gozo. Mainly, they deal with land- use planning and development issues as, they try to find a balance between economic social needs and the protection of the environment (MEPA, 2006). Whereas, the 1992 Structure Plan established an overall strategic framework for land use, local plans deal with area planning on a detailed basis and so, respond to local issues. Lastly, one should note that SPED is given the force of law. Chapter 552, of the laws of Malta, defines the structure plan as being law. Since, SPED is the predecessor of the 1992 Structure Plan, that makes SPED law as well (Chapter 552, 2016).

One mechanism in which law and policy work together to ensure environmental safeguard, is by having policies which lay down specific environmental safeguards, and a legal requirement that every environmental proposal has to follow. When one applies for development, one has to go through the relative policies and make sure that the development being proposed is in line with those specific policies. This may not be so easy since, our principle plan, the SPED, was made to protect current needs yet, local plans do not-considering that they are old, and were built on the 1992 structure plan. In fact, the eldest LP dates back to 1995, being the Marsaxlokk Bay LP (Planning Authority, 1995), whilst the most current dates back to 2006, being the South Malta LP (Planning Authority, 2006). A major difficulty that the PA faces today is that, the SPED establishes a strategy for planning to ensure sustainable development however, LPs are still regulated by a regime which was much more concerned with land use. Being out dated, LPs are still targeted towards that type of reasoning which may cause problems for the PA, for example outside development zones (ODZs) are not catered for by LPs. Therefore, there is a need to revise the LPs in order to ensure consistency between them and the SPED, and establish policies which are of far more strategic significance.

1.3 Examining the current Regulatory Framework and its effectiveness in:

1.3.1 Safeguarding and enhancing the Environment; preventing or decreasing Environmental crime

Environmental crime is a type of crime in which the offender endangers the physical safety or health of a person, as well as the environment, thus is subject to criminal prosecution since the person breached the law (Clifford & Edwards, 1998; Situ & Emmons, 2000). Such crimes are often portrayed as being victimless, however they are not (Luttenberger & Luttenberger, 2017). There are different forms of Environmental crime, which include in; illegal development, illegal dumping, overfishing, illegal hunting and hunting for protected species.

Let us take the example of illegal development. Imagine that a person has applied to build a two story house, with one pool and a garden. This type of development has been approved however, at construction phase the person decides to build the house with three stories, instead of the approved two. This is considered as being a breach of the law, because the house being built was not approved in that manner. The permit that was issued for the person was to build a house with only two stories. Considering that this person breeched the law, enforcement actions can take place since, the law lays down procedures to ensure adherence

6

to policy. Prior breaches of that policy, enforcement action will take place. In fact, Chapter 504 of the laws of Malta specifically states that "any person who carries out any development ... without a development permission, or of with a development permission, fails to comply ... [with the permit] shall be guilty of an offence against this Act" (Chapter 504, 2014, p. 48). Thus, since the person breeched the law, he/she is liable, on conviction, to a fine of not less than €1,500 and not more than €100,000, or/and even (not less than) 3 months to (not more than) 3 years of prison time (Chapter 504, 2014). Additionally, the court, besides giving the punishment necessary for the breech of law, can order the person to undo anything that was done without permission, which in this case is the third story of the house, or to change the house with the imposed conditions within a specific time frame (Chapter 504, 2014). Furthermore, failure to do so, the court which is representing the law, would give permission to the PA to take down the illegal building. The law gives a high level of power to the PA in order to act upon any illegal development, which is in any way breeching the law.

However, utilizing such enforcement actions is not always as easy as it may sound. This is because, although the law lays down specific procedures and policies, the law itself also provides certain mechanisms by which a person can contest enforcement notice. This is done because the law is intended to provide balance between, the rights exercised by the PA and the individual's rights of who owns that particular development. One example of such a mechanism is, the Environment and Planning Review Tribunal (EPRT). Chapter 551: Environment and Planning Review Tribunal Act, of the laws of Malta, states that the role of the EPRT is to review decisions of the PA and the decision of the ERA (Chapter 551, 2016). Hence, its primary role being to review planning and environmental decisions in terms of law (The Judiciary Portal, 2019). In fact, a case pertaining to the EPRT is as follows.

Back in the 80s, a person obtained a permit to develop a boundary wall on his ODZ field. The permit was issued with specific regulations saying that the boundary wall should be of a particular height. Yet, this individual ended up building a whole forte instead, and to top it off, he also built a villa which included in a swimming pool, amongst other things. Later, he had applied to sanction that particular villa, so he had informed the authorities about this illegal development. The villa was built on land which according to policy was ODZ. And so, even though he had applied to legalize it several times, it had always gotten refused. The authority gave the individual 15 days to comply with the law, however he did not. This means that the authority had the right to institute enforcement procedures. He applied against the case, stating that the authority was going against Article 8 of the European Convention on Human rights, which provides the right to respect for one's private and family life (European Convention on Human Rights, n.d.). By taking away the villa, the person's family would become homeless and this goes against Article 8. In this case, authority gave the right for this villa to remain, given the person's age and other several circumstances.

Another interesting case that took place in the U.K. back in 2001 was Chapman v. The United Kingdom, with application number 27238/95 ("Chapman", 2001). In brief, the people concerned in the case were the Chapmans, who were the owners of a piece of land purchased in 1985. Caravans were sited in an area which was referred to as being an ODZ area, as it was a countryside. They were sited within the area, without the necessary permits, and the authorities executed enforcement procedures so as to have the caravans removed from site. One should note that these caravans were used by the owners with the intention of being their home since, they were sleeping in it. Long story short, the owners appealed the case to the European Court on Human rights, as they claimed that by taking away the caravans, it would go against Article 8 (European Convention on Human Rights, n.d.). The court did not only base its judgment on the fact that the caravans were cited in the area without a permit (and so, just like our local law states, that every development has to happen upon an issue of a permit), it was also based on the fact that they were sited on an area which was found to have ecological significance. Hence, the court found no violation of Article 8, even though they took into account that the caravans were like a home to the owners. They were given a particular time frame in which they had to remove the caravans from site, however they did not and so, the authority had to take actions of its own ("Chapman", 2001).

Moreover, illegal development is only one example of environmental crime. Over fishing and illegal hunting, also raise concerns with regards to this type of crime. Over fishing is an environmental activity, i.e. what we refer to as the fish farms, not the day-to-day activity that individuals practice as a hobby. The structure of such fish farms, being the cages that compose the fish farms, are also considered as being development. Development at sea also falls under Chapter 552, of the laws of Malta, since it defines development as both development on land and sea (Chapter 552, 2016). Safeguarding protected species also contribute to the protection of the environment as, it falls under the law of Chapter 549, of the laws of Malta. That being the subsidiary law of Chapter 549.120: Species protection (designation of national species) regulations, which applies provisions to safeguard the protection of species (Chapter 549.120, 2018).

1.3.2 Ensuring the Sustainable Development of Malta's urban, rural, costal and marine area

In order for present and future generations to enjoy such a planet, development needs to be sustainable. This means that development that occurs, accommodates the needs of the present generation, without damaging the ability for those future generations to accommodate their own needs, within the environment (Rogers, Jalal, & Boyd, 2008; National Environment Policy, 2012; Elliott, 2013). Within the SPED policy, there are found several policies regarding the urban, rural, costal and marine areas within the Maltese Islands towards a more sustainable development since, it lays down a number of policies which tackle environmental protection (SPED, 2015). The law lays down an obligation amongst the PA in every decision which it awards, that it must always apply plans and policies. This is because the relative plans and policies lay down a number of environmental safeguards. One of which is; thematic objective one- "to manage the available potential space and environmental resources [both] on land and sea sustainably" (SPED, 2015, p. 20).

Another environmental safeguard which falls under SPED is thematic objective six- "to safeguard environmental health from air and noise pollution and risks associated with use and management of chemicals" (SPED, 2015, p. 21). A case related to this is as follows. Imagine, that a person has a villa area and has a garage situated within that area, characterized by a number of open spaces. The person submits a planning application with regards to the change of use for the garage, to become a shop in an area where, thematic objective six applies. The PA will review that application with relevance to the policies. However, this type of development will generate noise and air pollution and so, the application was refused by the PA since, it goes against the relative policy.

In addition, I feel that the current regulatory framework within the local context, is effective at safeguarding the environment. Even tough at times, it did not always manage to. Every case is different, and given that the law provides certain mechanisms in which a person can contest a case, I understand that at times it is hard for the authority to utilize such enforcement. The situation, is constantly improving yet, I do feel that further work needs to be done, such as raise more awareness about safeguarding the environment. Harsher punishments can act as a deterrence against such crimes. So, maybe introducing them is not such a bad idea. However, firstly, what needs to be done is review the laws and policies again and amend them according to the current needs and situations, since we have some which are out dated, like for instance the LPs. Tough, in general, I feel that it is effective (Muscat, 2015).

1.4 Conclusion

In conclusion, environmental crimes are becoming more and more common every day, and so requiring more attention. Ironically enough, more people are committing such crimes yet, only a few of them are actually being caught and punished (Luttenberger & Luttenberger, 2017). There needs to be further awareness about safeguarding and protecting the environment, not only for the benefit of present human beings but, also for future generations. Moreover, for such laws and policies to work, they not only need to be well-designed and implemented, but also enforced (Gunningham, 2011). It is useless having this legislation, if such crimes are not going to be sanctioned.

References

Betz, S. (2016). The importance of protecting our environment: temperatures are rising while optimism for the future is on the decline. *Odyssey.* Retrieved January 18, 2019 from https://www.theodysseyonline.com/importance-protecting-environment

Bing-Yuk, R. T. (2009, March 19). Who should be mainly responsible for protecting the environment? (i.e. the government? Scientists?...). *South China morning post.* Retrieved January 18, 2019 from https://www.scmp.com/article/673756/who- should-be-mainly-responsible-protecting-environment-ie-government-scientists

Chapman v. The United Kingdom (Application no. 27238/95). (2001). *ESCR-Net.* Retrieved from https://www.escr-net.org/caselaw/2008/chapman-v-united-kingdom-application-no-2723895?fbclid=IwAR2BXa7TtL-fWxE0mrDM7NrMkBHaNyoQjz8n48UZyQOXw1M2KRkfmd6AgmY

Chapter 504: Environment and Development Planning Act 2014. Laws of Malta. Retrieved from http://www.justiceservices.gov.mt/downloaddocument.aspx?app=lom&itemid=114 07&l=1

Chapter 549: Environment Protection Act 2016. Laws of Malta. Retrieved from http://www.justiceservices.gov.mt/DownloadDocument.aspx?app=lom&itemid=124 46&l=1

Chapter 549.120: Species protection (designation of national species) regulations 2018. Laws of Malta. Retrieved from http://www.justiceservices.gov.mt/DownloadDocument.aspx?app=lom&itemid=127 86&l=1

Chapter 551: Environment and Planning Review Tribunal Act 2016. Laws of Malta. Retrieved from http://www.justiceservices.gov.mt/DownloadDocument.aspx?app=lom&itemid=124 50&l=1

Chapter 552: Development Planning Act 2016. Laws of Malta. Retrieved from
http://justiceservices.gov.mt/DownloadDocument.aspx?app=lom&itemid=12451&l=
1

Clifford, M., & Edwards, T. D. (1998). Chapter 1: Defining "Environmental Crime". In,
Clifford, M., *Environmental Crime: Enforcement, policy, and social responsibility,*
pp. 5-27.

Retrieved from https://books.google.com.mt/books?id=wddxPK-
0O20C&pg=PA172&dq=type+of+environmental+crime&hl=en&sa=X&ved=0ahUK
Ewi
J7oGuk_jfAhUJWSwKHf01DdYQ6AEILDAB#v=onepage&q=type%20of%20envir
onme ntal%20crime&f=false

Elliot, J. A. (2013). What is sustainable development. In, *An introduction to sustainable
development* (4th Ed.), pp. 8-56. Retrieved from
https://books.google.com.mt/books?id=ZebfCgAAQBAJ&printsec=frontcover&dq=s
u
stainable+development&hl=en&sa=X&ved=0ahUKEwiElae84_7fAhUDiywKHXFh
D4gQ 6AEIJzAA#v=onepage&q=sustainable%20development&f=false

ERA (Environment and Resources Authority). (2014). Strategic plan for the Environment and
Development. Retrieved from https://era.org.mt/en/Pages/Strategic-Plan-for-the-
Environment--Development.aspx

ERA (Environment and Resources Authority). (n.d.). Legislation under Environment
Protection Act (CAP 549). Retrieved from
https://eracms.gov.mt/en/Pages/Legislation%20under%20Environment%20Protecti
on%20Act%20(CAP%20549).aspx

European Convention on Human Rights. (n.d.). Retrieved from
https://www.echr.coe.int/Documents/Convention_ENG.pdf

Gunningham, N. (2011). Enforcing environmental regulation. *Journal of Environmental Law,*
23(2), 169-201. Doi:10.1093/jel/eqr006

Kiyoung, K. (2014). The relationship between the law and public policy: Is it a chi-square or normative shape for the policy makers. *Social Sciences, 3*(4), 137-143. Retrieved from

https://www.researchgate.net/publication/268632630_The_relationship_between_the_law_and_public_policy_Is_it_a_chi-square_or_normative_shape_for_the_policy_makers

Luttenberger, A., & Luttenberger, L. R. (2017). Challenges in regulating Environmental Crimes [PDF file]. *IMSC (International Maritime Science Conference)*. Retrieved from

https://bib.irb.hr/datoteka/871672.IMSC2017_Luttenberger_and_Runko_Luttenberger.pdf

MEPA. (2006, October 7). Local plans for the Maltese Islands: What is a local plan? *Times of Malta.* Retrieved January 20, 2019 from

https://www.timesofmalta.com/articles/view/20061007/opinion/local-plans-for- the-maltese-islands.39229

Muscat, C. (2015, April 9). 185 cases of illegal development addressed in two months-MEPA. *Times of Malta.* Retrieved January 21, 2019 from

https://www.timesofmalta.com/articles/view/20150409/local/185-cases-of-illegal-development-addressed-in-two-months-mepa.563313

National Environment Policy. (2012). Retrieved from

https://msdec.gov.mt/en/decc/Documents/environment/National%20Environment%20Policy.pdf

Planning Authority. (1995). Local plan details: Marsaxlokk Bay local plan. Retrieved from

https://www.pa.org.mt/en/local-plan-details/marsaxlokk-bay-local-plan

Planning Authority. (2006). Local plan details: South Malta local plan. Retrieved from

https://www.pa.org.mt/en/local-plan-details/south-malta-local-plan

Planning Authority. (2015). Strategic plan details: strategic plan for environment and development. Retrieved from https://www.pa.org.mt/en/strategic-plan-details/strategic%20plan%20for%20the%20environment%20and%20development

Planning Authority. (2016, November 29). Vision, mission, values [Video file]. Retrieved from https://www.youtube.com/watch?v=yoL6zvhD0L4&feature=youtu.be

Rogers, P. P., Jalal, K. F., & Boyd, J. A. (2008). From Malthus to sustainable development. In, *An introduction to sustainable development*, pp. 20-39. Retrieved from https://books.google.com.mt/books?id=GZ4Pvk0LVQMC&printsec=frontcover&dq=s
ustainable+development&hl=en&sa=X&ved=0ahUKEwiElae84_7fAhUDiywKHXFh
D4g Q6AEILTAB#v=onepage&q=sustainable%20development&f=false

Situ, Y., & Emmons, D. (2000). Introduction. In, *Environmental crime: The Criminal Justice system's role in protecting the Environment*, pp. 1-18. Retrieved from https://books.google.com.mt/books?id=qww5DQAAQBAJ&printsec=frontcover&dq
=
what+is+environmental+crime&hl=en&sa=X&ved=0ahUKEwjgo6bgk_jfAhXBkCw
KHX
VYAdwQ6AEINTAD#v=onepage&q=what%20is%20environmental%20crime&f=fa
lse

SPED (Strategic Plan for Environment and Development). (2015). Retrieved from http://extwprlegs1.fao.org/docs/pdf/mlt158315.pdf?fbclid=IwAR2GUcD-
s98lD7vi1EmTlKMskM0P0iJnUiq7mv4ooNaYr--yfO9YldTK1qU

Split of MEPA into two independent authorities comes into effect. (2017, May 9). *TVM News*. Retrieved January 19, 2019 from https://www.tvm.com.mt/en/news/split-of-mepa- into-two-independent-authorities-comes-into-effect/

The Judiciary Portal. (2019). EPRT. Retrieved January 21, 2019 from http://www.eprt.org.mt/en/eprt

YOUR KNOWLEDGE HAS VALUE